DISCARD

"WHY DO WE HAVE TO MOVE?"

Copyright © 1996 by Cynthia MacGregor

A Lyle Stuart Book
Published by Carol Publishing Group
Lyle Stuart is a registered trademark of Carol Communications, Inc.

Editorial, sales and distribution, rights and permissions inquiries should be addressed to Carol Publishing Group, 120 Enterprise Avenue, Secaucus, NJ 07094

Carol Publishing Group books may be purchased in bulk at special discounts for sales promotion, fund-raising, or educational purposes. Special editions can be created to specifications. For details, contact Special Sales Department, 120 Enterprise Avenue, Secaucus, N.J. 07094.

Manufactured in the United States of America
12 11 10 9 8 7 6 5 4 3 2 1

Library of Congress Cataloging-in-Publication Data

MacGregor, Cynthia.
    Why do we have to move? : helping your child adjust—with love and illustrations / Cynthia MacGregor : illustrated by David Clark.
        p.   cm.
    "A Lyle Stuart book."
    ISBN 0-8184-0583-X (hardcover)
    1. Moving, Household—Psychological aspects.   2. Child psychology.
3. Parent and child.   I. Clark, David, 1960-   II. Title.
TX307.M33 1996
648'.9'019—dc20   96-26092
                                                               CIP

"WHY DO WE HAVE TO MOVE?"

Helping your child adjust—with love and illustrations

CYNTHIA MacGREGOR
ILLUSTRATIONS BY DAVID CLARK

Published by Carol Publishing Group

Do you like new things and new experiences?

It's fun getting a new toy, isn't it? It's fun because it's different from the other things you've already played with so many times.

But wait—maybe your mom said, "Your birthday is coming soon. You'll be getting a bunch of new toys. It's time to get rid of some of the old ones."

So maybe you had to give away some toys before getting new ones for your birthday. It's a little hard to get rid of old things, isn't it? But it's not so bad when you think about getting new things in their place.

Why?

Because it's <u>fun</u> to try something new.

It's fun to try a new toy. It's fun to meet a new friend or go to a new playground.

There was a time when you had never eaten a hot dog. (Yes, really!) But then you tried one for the first time. And I'll bet you love hot dogs now.

You may have been scared the first time your mom or dad pushed you in a swing or helped you slide down a slide. But don't you love swings and slides now?

You didn't always know the kids who are now your friends. At one time they were strangers. But now you really enjoy playing with them (even though you probably fight over toys and other things sometimes).

New experiences can be fun. And until you've eaten a new food, or met a new friend, or played with a new toy, you don't know how much you're going to like it.

Are you ready for another new experience? A <u>big</u> one? You're going to live someplace new!

It's a big change. But changes can be very exciting. Just like with food and friends and toys, you never know how great something new can be till you try it.

Like hot dogs.

And ice cream cones.

Or your best friend.

Or your favorite toy.

A "family room" is a "fun room."

There are lots of reasons families move. I can't tell you all of them. That would take too long. But here are some of the most common reasons:

Many people want a larger house.

Maybe now you have to share a bedroom with your brother or sister. After you move, you might have a room of your own.

The new house might have something called a "family room," too. A family room usually doesn't have to be kept quite as neat as a living room. (It's funny, you can usually do more living—more playing, more horsing around, more making a mess—in a family room than in a living room.)

Sometimes a family that lives in an apartment decides to move to a house.

There are some neat things about living in an apartment. Like being able to visit a friend who lives in the building without having to put on your raincoat when it's raining or your snowsuit when it's really cold out.

But you can't make too much noise, because you might annoy the neighbors. Maybe your mom has said, "Don't jump. That will disturb the neighbors downstairs," or "Don't play your music so loud. That will bother the neighbors next door."

In a house, you don't have to worry as much about bothering the neighbors. There will probably be houses on either side of yours, so, of course, you need to be considerate of the people who live there. (No screaming and yelling in the yard early on a Sunday morning.) But you don't have to be nearly as careful.

Also, many apartment buildings don't have backyards. And if they do, the yard doesn't belong to just one family. Most houses have backyards, and if yours does you will have all of that space just for you and your family and whoever you invite to your house. You might have to share it with squirrels, robins, and bunny rabbits, though!

Another reason for moving is when a family wants to live in a whole different town.

Perhaps your dad or mom has gotten a new job in a different city. Then the whole family has to move to where the job is.

Sometimes people want to live in a neighborhood they like better.

Maybe your neighborhood isn't as nice as it used to be. Or maybe your parents couldn't afford to live in a nicer neighborhood before, but they can now. They want the best for you. They want you to live in the nicest, safest neighborhood they can find.

Or maybe the school in the new neighborhood is better than the one you go to now. Your mom and dad want you to go to a great school with good teachers and nice kids. Usually what school you go to depends on where you live—so to go to a better one, you may have to move.

Those aren't all the reasons people move. But they're the most common ones.

Your mom or dad can tell you what their reason is for moving. But it's interesting to know what other people's reasons are, too.

If you live in a neighborhood of apartments, there are probably signs in front of some of the buildings that say APARTMENT FOR RENT. If you live in a neighborhood of houses, there are probably FOR SALE signs in front of some of the houses. These houses and apartments are available to rent or buy because somebody has moved, or is going to.

There are *lots* of people looking for someplace new to live.

If you watch out your car window, you'll see moving vans loaded with furniture and clothes and kids' toys and bikes. Ask your mom or dad to start pointing out moving vans to you. You'll be surprised at how many there are. People are moving from house to house every day.

Sometimes they just move across the street.

Sometimes they move across town.

Sometimes they move clear across the country.

Your mom or dad can tell you how far it is to where you're going to move. Look on a map and see.

"Is anybody else moving to Elm Street?"

It's a lot like chocolate and spinach.

You might like to eat nothing but candy and ice cream and chocolate cake. You'd probably love it if you never had to eat spinach or Brussels sprouts or squash or the other foods you don't love as much as your favorites. But you know that you <u>need</u> to eat healthy foods.

You do sometimes get to eat foods you really love, like cookies or hamburgers or spaghetti and meatballs.

You also eat some foods you like, even if you don't love them. Maybe you feel that way about chicken or baked potatoes or soup.

And you have to eat some foods even if you don't like them, because they keep your body healthy.

But what does all this have to do with moving? Well, moving is like that, too. It's part chocolate and part spinach. There are things about moving that you'll love, and there are things about moving that you won't like at all.

If you're moving nearby, you'll still be able to visit all your friends. Of course, if your best friend lives right next door to you now, that won't be the case after you move.

But there will be new kids in your new neighborhood.

If you're moving nearby, you can still see all your old friends, <u>and</u> you'll make new friends, too.

If you're moving farther away, you won't be able to see your old friends regularly like you do now. But even though you don't play together anymore, you can still be their friend.

A new neighborhood means new friends—and surprises.

You can write each other letters. If you're too young to read and write, you can tell your mom and dad what you want to say in a letter, and they'll write it down for you. Imagine the fun of coming home from school and finding you've got mail from one of your old friends!

<u>You can talk on the phone.</u> If you've moved far from your old town, you can call your best friends once in a while. Calling someplace far away costs money. But your parents will probably let you call some of your old friends from time to time, so that you can keep in touch. You might want to tell them what moving is like and describe your new home and new friends.

You might even be able to visit each other. Maybe you'll move too far away to go over to your friends' houses after school but near enough that once in a long while your parents can drive you back to your old town and leave you at one of your friends' houses for the weekend. Or your friends can come and visit you over a long weekend.

Even if you move far away, your family might decide to take an airplane and fly to your old town to visit friends.

If you're in school—or in preschool—you'll probably be changing schools.

If this sounds like more "spinach and chocolate," you're right. The "spinach" part is that you'll have to get used to a new school, new friends, and a new teacher. Anything new takes getting used to.

The "chocolate" part is that it's going to be a surprise. And surprises are usually fun. You don't know what the teacher is going to be like, but maybe you'll like him or her even better than you like your teacher now. You don't know what the school is like, but maybe it's newer, or better, or nicer in some other way. You'll miss your old school friends, but you'll meet new kids who will become good friends.

Even if you miss your old school, you'll find some things you like better about the new school. What are they? I really don't know. But you'll find out.

Surprise!

That's another thing about moving that's more like chocolate than spinach. Your new neighborhood and your new house are bound to have some things about them that you'll like a lot. And many will be surprises.

Your mom or dad can tell you now about some of those nice things in your new house and your new neighborhood. They might be things like:

Ducks in a pond nearby

An attic you can play in

 Being near a relative you don't get to see much of now

 A neighbor who will bake yummy chocolate-chip cookies just for you

 A tree with a bird's nest in it

 An ice cream truck that comes right past your door in warm weather

 A tree in your backyard in which your dad can build a treehouse

🍫 A firehouse really close by

🍫 Your new best friend, living right next door

🍫 Write one of your surprises here when you find it!

My Surprise is....

_____

_____

_____

What else is "spinach" about moving?

Your mom might ask you to give away some toys before you move. The fewer things you have to move, the easier moving is and the less it costs.

It's hard to pack up all your stuff and see your room full of nothing except boxes.

The new house might seem strange when you first move in, and you will probably feel homesick at first. But you'll quickly begin to feel more comfortable.

What else is "chocolate" about moving?

Chocolate You might get some new furniture or toys when you move.

Chocolate Your new house (or apartment) is going to have all kinds of wonderful new places to hide when you play hide 'n' seek.

Chocolate Is there anything you <u>don't</u> like about the house and neighborhood where you live now? Is there a kid down the street who's kind of mean? Is there a tree branch outside that makes scary noises when it rubs against your window in the wind? When you move, you get to leave all that behind!

Moving is like a surprise package. Till you open it, you don't know what's inside—or how much you're going to enjoy it.

Surprise! Maybe there's a hill around the corner from the new house that's just perfect for wintertime sledding.

Surprise! Maybe there's a spot where you can grow your very own flower garden.

Surprise! Maybe the window of your new bedroom looks out on a tree and right into a squirrel's hiding hole.

"Hi! How do *you* like this neighborhood?"

Or maybe those aren't your surprises. What are they, then? I don't know. Neither do you, yet. (If you did, they wouldn't be surprises!) But you'll find out.

Here's what you need to know most of all:

Whether or not you're moving nearby...

And whether or not you have to leave your old friends behind...

And whether or not you're changing schools...

And even though you're leaving your old, familiar, comfortable home...

...the really important stuff is going with you.

• If you have pets, they will almost definitely be going with you.

• Even if you have to leave a few toys behind, most of your toys—certainly your favorite ones—are going with you.

• Unless the move is because of a divorce, your whole family is going with you. (This means your parents and your brothers and sisters.)

• Since your family is moving with you, your new home will be filled with all the love and warm feelings you have now.

And since we know your parents have a good reason for moving, they'll probably be happier in the new house. And most likely you'll be happier there, too.

Moving is an adventure.

Enjoy it!